Our Senses

SIGHT

Kay Woodward

GARETH**STEVENS**
PUBLISHING
A World Almanac Education Group Company

Please visit our web site at: **www.garethstevens.com**
**For a free color catalog describing Gareth Stevens Publishing's
list of high-quality books and multimedia programs, call
1-800-542-2595 (USA) or 1-800-387-3178 (Canada).
Gareth Stevens Publishing's fax: (414) 332-3567.**

Library of Congress Cataloging-in-Publication Data

Woodward, Kay.
    Sight / Kay Woodward.
        p. cm — (Our senses)
    Includes index.
    ISBN 0-8368-4407-6 (lib. bdg.)
    1. Vision—Juvenile literature.   I. Title.
QP475.7.W65   2005
612.8'4—dc22   2004052569

This North American edition first published in 2005 by
Gareth Stevens Publishing
A World Almanac Education Group Company
330 West Olive Street, Suite 100
Milwaukee, Wisconsin 53212 USA

This U.S. edition copyright © 2005 by Gareth Stevens, Inc.
Original edition copyright © 2005 by Hodder Wayland.
First published in 2005 by Hodder Wayland, an imprint of
Hodder Children's Books, a division of Hodder Headline
Limited, 338 Euston Road, London NW1 3BH, U.K.

Commissioning Editor: Victoria Brooker
Book Editor: Katie Sergeant
Consultant: Carol Ballard
Picture Research: Katie Sergeant
Book Designer: Jane Hawkins
Cover: Hodder Children's Books

Gareth Stevens Editor: Barbara Kiely Miller
Gareth Stevens Designer: Kami Koenig

Printed in China

1 2 3 4 5 6 7 8 9 09 08 07 06 05

Picture Credits
Archie Miles: 12; Ardea: 19 (Jim Zipp); Corbis: imprint page,
13 (Jack Hollingsworth), 4 (Tom and Dee Ann McCarthy),
7 (Royalty-Free), 9 (Earl & Nazima Kowall), 11 (FK Photo),
14 (Ariel Skelley), 21 (Gallo Images/Anthony Bannister);
FLPA: 20 (B.B. Casals); Getty Images: cover (The Image
Bank/Pete Atkinson), title page (Stone/Patrisha Thomson),
8 (Taxi/David Leahy), 10 (Stone/Pascal Crapet); Martyn F.
Chillmaid 16, 17; NaturePl.com: 18 (Lynn M. Stone/Royalty-
Free); Wayland Picture Library: 5, 15. The artwork on page
6 is by Peter Bull, and the artwork on pages 22 and 23
is by Jane Hawkins.

About the Author

Kay Woodward is an experienced children's author who
has written over twenty nonfiction and fiction titles.

About the Consultant

Carol Ballard is an elementary school science
coordinator. She is the author of many books for
children and is a consultant for several publishers.

CONTENTS

Words in **bold** type can be found in the glossary.

LOOK AROUND!

The world is filled with many objects, colors, and shapes. Some are light and bright. Others are dull and dark. Some move, and some stay still.

A merry-go-round is full of moving color.

Our **sense** of **sight** allows us to see the many amazing things around us. We use our eyes to see.

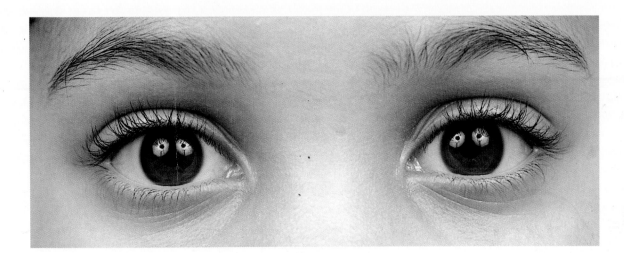

The colored part of your eye is called the iris.
The black center is a hole in the iris, called the pupil.

HOW YOUR EYES WORK

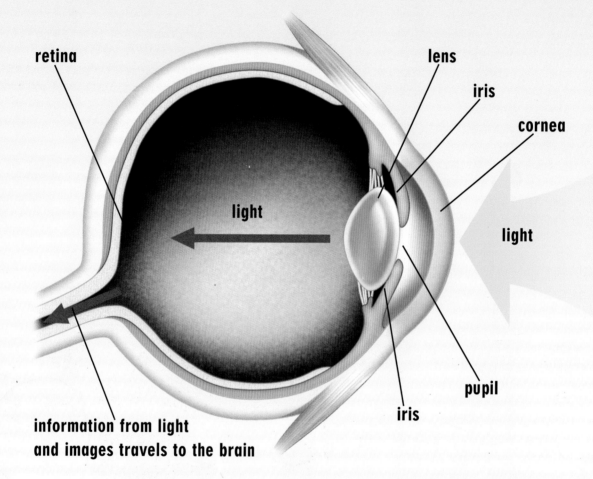

retina

lens

iris

cornea

light

light

information from light
and images travels to the brain

iris

pupil

This is what an eye looks like from the inside.

Light bounces off an object and enters your eyes, giving information about the object's shape and color. An upside-down **image** of the object is formed on the **retina**. The image is then sent to your brain, which forms an image that is right-side-up and tells you what the object is. This is how you see things.

Each of your eyes gives you a slightly different view of an object. Hold an object in front of your face. First, shut only your left eye, then shut only your right eye. Can you see the difference?

Your brain puts the views from your two eyes together.

This helps you know how near or far away objects are.

LIGHT AND DARKNESS

Pupils get smaller in bright light.

Light enters your eyes through their **pupils**. Your **irises** have muscles that change the size of the pupils to let the right amount of light into your eyes. In bright light, pupils get smaller so that too much light does not enter the eyes.

Pupils get bigger in darkness.

When there is darkness or little light, pupils get bigger. When pupils are bigger, more light enters the eyes, and you can see better.

TEARS AND BLINKING

Tears come from tiny holes, or ducts, near the corner of each eye. When we are hurt or upset, tears come out of our tear ducts.

We blink our eyes thousands of times every day.
Blinking keeps eyes clean, healthy, and wet.

CLEAR OR FUZZY?

The **lens**, near the front of the eye, **focuses** the light that enters the eye. If the lens is the right shape, objects look clear. If the lens is longer, shorter, thinner, or wider, objects look fuzzy.

clear image   fuzzy image

Some people have perfect eyesight, but many people need **glasses** to help them see clearly.

SEEING CLEARLY

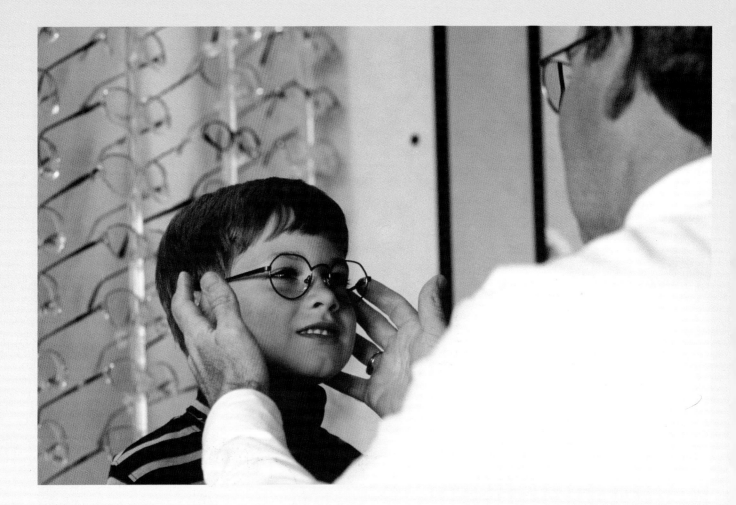

An optometrist is a doctor who tests how well people can see. The optometrist will put different lenses in front of your eyes until finding the lens that helps you see the best. An optician then makes the correct lenses for your pair of glasses.

Many people like to wear contact lenses instead of glasses. Contact lenses are small pieces of plastic that are placed on the **cornea** of each eye.

People who wear contact lenses
need to keep them very clean.

BLINDNESS

People who are blind are not able to see. Some people are blind when they are born. Others become blind because of an injury or illness. Some people lose their sight in only one eye.

Guide dogs are specially trained to help people who are blind.

Braille is a type of writing made of raised dots that are arranged in different patterns. The patterns stand for letters and other characters. People who are blind read by touching the dots with their fingers.

ANIMALS AND SIGHT

Cats can see the smallest movements in the darkness.

Some animals see differently than people see.
Many sharks can see only in black and white.
Cats' eyes can see well in the darkness or in
very little light.

Hawks have excellent eyesight.
As they swoop through the air,
hawks can see small animals
far below them.

A hawk flies high above the ground, looking for prey.

INSECTS AND SIGHT

Spiders, which are animals related to insects, have eight eyes. They can see out of the back, the front, and the sides of their heads — all at the same time!

With their eight eyes, spiders can be hard to catch.

Some insects, such as butterflies and dragonflies, have only two eyes, but each eye is made up of lots of smaller eyes. Information from all of the smaller eyes is sent to the insect's brain to form one picture.

CAN YOU BELIEVE WHAT YOU SEE?

Optical illusions are images that trick the eyes and the brain. What do you see in the following pictures?

1. Is this picture a vase or two faces?

Answer: This picture shows a vase — and two faces! Can you see a light-blue vase? Look at the picture again and see if you can spot two dark-blue faces.

2. Are the purple lines curved or straight?

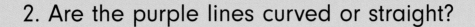

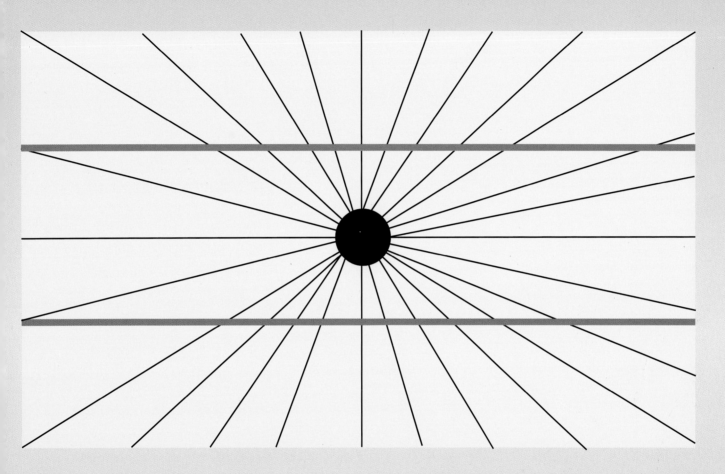

Answer: The purple lines may look as if they are curved, but if you hold a ruler beside them, you will see that they are straight. Your eyes have been tricked by the round, black spot and the thin, black lines.

GLOSSARY

cornea: the clear, outer part of the eye that covers the iris and the pupil

focuses: adjusts light to produce a clear picture

glasses: a pair of glass or plastic lenses held in front of the eyes by a frame. Glasses are also called eyeglasses.

image: a picture of an object formed by a device such as a lens or a mirror

irises: the colored parts of the eyes that adjust the size of the pupils

lens: a clear, curved object that focuses light. The lens inside the eye focuses light to form a picture on the retina.

pupils: the center holes in the irises through which light enters the eyes

retina: the back of the eye, where an upside-down picture of an object is formed before being sent to the brain for identification

sense: a natural ability to receive and process information using one or more of the body's sense organs, such as the ears, eyes, nose, tongue, or skin. The five senses are hearing, sight, smell, taste, and touch.

sight: the ability to see and identify the location, color, and shape of objects

INDEX